FABER EARLY ORGAN SER

European Organ Music of the 16th & 17th C
Series Editor : James Dalton

Volume 4

Spain & Portugal

c.1550-1620

CARREIRA · PAIVA · BERMUDO · PALERO
SANTA MARÍA · CABEZÓN · RODRIGUES COELHO

EDITED BY
JAMES DALTON

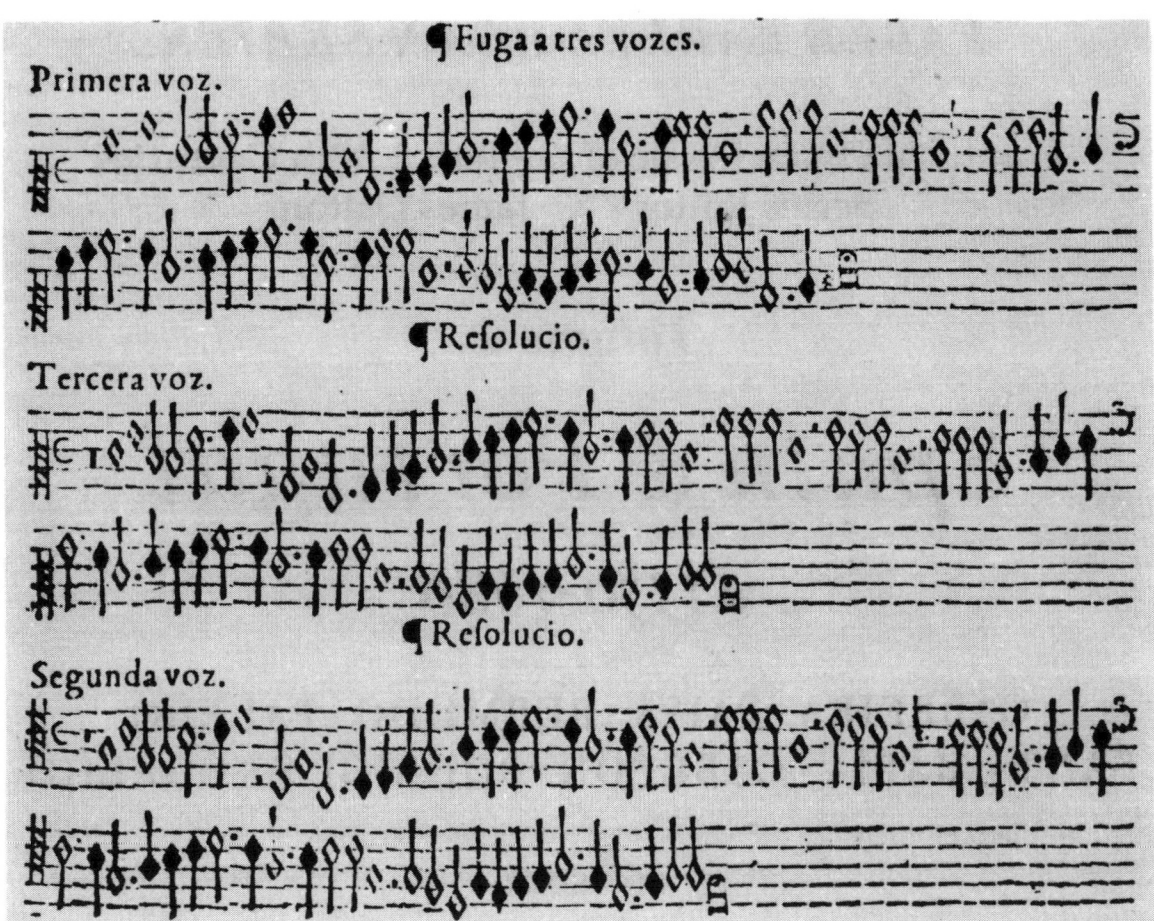

Tomás de Santa María, Libro llamado Arte de tañer Fantasía (1565),
lower half of f.68, showing the three separate parts of the Fuga a tres voces

© 1987 by Faber Music Ltd
First published in 1987 by Faber Music Ltd
Bloomsbury House
74–77 Great Russell Street
London WC1B 3DA
Music engraved by Christopher Hinkins
Cover design by M & S Tucker
Cover illustration by John Brennan
German translations by and Ursula Riniker
Printed in England by Caligraving Ltd
All rights reserved

ISBN10: 0-571-50774-3
EAN13: 978-0-571-50774-0

Editor and publisher gratefully acknowledge financial assistance from
The Queen's College, University of Oxford, the Faculty of Music, University of Oxford, and the Leverhulme Foundation.
Access to sources used in the preparation of this volume was by kind permission of the following libraries:
Biblioteca pública e arquivo distrital; Braga, Biblioteca geral, Universidade de Coimbra; Biblioteca nacional, madrid.
Thanks also go to Bernadette Nelson and Dr. Macario Santiago Kastner for valuable guidance on musical and liturgical matters.

To buy Faber Music publications or to find out about the full range of titles available
please contact your local music retailer or Faber Music sales enquiries:

Faber Music Limited, Burnt Mill, Elizabeth Way, Harlow, CM20 2HX England
Tel: +44 (0)1279 82 89 82   Fax: +44 (0)1279 82 89 83
sales@fabermusic.com   fabermusicstore.com

Contents – Inhalt

Editorial Procedure *p. iv* Anmerkung des Herausgebers *S.vi*
Introduction *p. iv* Vorwort *S.vii*
The Church Modes *p. v* Die kirklichen Modi *S.viii*
Ornamentation *p. vi* Ornamentierung *S.ix*
Registration *p. vi* Registrierung *S.ix*

1 · Tento do 8° tom *António Carreira (c.1525–c.1589)*	2
2 · Tento do 3° tom *Heliadorus de Paiva (c.1500–1552)*	6
3 · Tento do 4° tom *Heliadorus de Paiva*	8
4 · Veni creator spiritus *Juan Bermudo (c.1510–?1565)*	10
5 · Pange lingua *Juan Bermudo*	11
6 · Tiento de 5° tono *Anonymous (1557)*	12
7 · Tiento de 7° tono super Philomena *Francisco Fernández Palero (d.1597)*	13
8 · Del modo de tañer a corcheas *Tomás de Santa María (d.?1570)*	15
9 · Fuga a dos voces *Tomás de Santa María*	16
10 · Fuga a tres voces *Tomás de Santa María*	16
11 · Fuga a cuatro voces *Tomás de Santa María*	17
12 · Beata viscera Mariae virginis *Antonio de Cabezón (1510–1566)*	18
13 · Versos del 8° tono de Magnificat *Antonio de Cabezón*	21
14 · Tiento sobre Cum sancto spiritu *Antonio de Cabezón*	25
15 · Versos do 3° tom *Manuel Rodrigues Coelho (c.1555–1635)*	27
16 · Tento do 2° tom *Manuel Rodrigues Coelho*	32

Critical Commentary *p. 40*

Editorial Procedure

This is a practical performing edition. All the pieces are presented in modern staff notation using treble and bass clefs. Within this arrangement, as much information as possible about the original sources is included on the score – considerably more, in some cases, than is found in other modern editions. The result, however, is not a facsimile in easy clefs; the editorial method that has been evolved is summarised as follows:

1. Unless otherwise indicated, original note-values, bar-lines, key-signatures and time-signatures have been preserved, and the distribution of notes between the staves retained (in final chords, original note-values have been preserved even where not every part has the same number of beats.) Owing to the use of modern staves and clefs, original stem directions have sometimes been altered, but an attempt has been made to retain the idiomatic free-voiced appearance of the original notation. Pieces notated in tablature, open score or separate parts have been transcribed onto two staves.
2. Original clefs and/or notation are indicated at the beginning of each piece, and at other points where necessary. Where a time-signature or proportion-sign occurring in the course of a piece has been altered, the original is shown between the staves.
3. Where unusual notation (e.g. black semibreves, white demi-semi-minims) appears in the original, it has been changed to a modern equivalent and noted in the Commentary.
4. Note-values extending over bar-lines have been transcribed using ties; otherwise, original note-groupings (unconventional beaming of quavers included) have generally been preserved. Although this can produce the appearance of inconsistency, there is often a purpose to the original script, and alteration in some cases but not in others would produce a confused picture. The only exceptions concern early sources in which each quaver or semiquaver has a separate tail, and tablature notation, for which a straightforward, conventional routine (for example, beaming semiquavers in groups of four) has been employed.
5. Accidentals have been reproduced in full as they occur in the sources, except that, where applicable, sharps and flats have been replaced by modern naturals (for example, f♮ is often given as f♭ in the original, and b♮ as b♯). Normally, an original accidental applies only to one note and immediate repetitions of it; where it appears to hold good for longer than this, no editorial marking has been added, and the modern convention of an accidental being effective for the remainder of the bar applies (the same convention applies in the case of accidentals supplied editorially). All editorial accidentals are given at full size in square brackets, except for cancelling accidentals in tablature notation, which are not strictly speaking editorial, since every note has its own symbol; these are therefore left unbracketed. Some editorial accidentals are essential because of the different conventions governing old and modern notation, while others are suggestions; the types can be distinguished by context.
6. Editorial ornaments, notes, rests and other details are given in square brackets. Ties added editorially are shown as ⌢. Editorial bar-lines are left unjoined between the staves, while in the occasional case of re-barring, the original bar-lines are given in heavy type above the stave. The interpolation of a longer or shorter bar should not be seen as invalidating the underlying rhythmic flow. Original indications of part-movement have been retained; editorial indications are shown by broken lines.
7. For any piece appearing in more than one source, a main source has been chosen. It appears at the top of the list of sources for that piece in the Commentary, and its text is regarded as basic. Any deviations from it (where, for instance, corrections have been made by the editor or where another source provides a superior reading) are noted in the Commentary. No attempt has been made to provide an exhaustive list of variants in additional sources.
8. A title has been provided at the head of each piece. Where titles and ascriptions are given in the sources, they are noted, in their original spellings, in the Commentary.

Introduction

Strong liturgical elements influenced the character of Iberian organ music of the sixteenth and seventeenth centuries. The function of the organist, as laid down in many church and cathedral ceremonial ordinances, was to play *alternatim* with the choir – that is, one verse was sung to plainchant, the next played on the organ, and so on – and in most of the main sources from Cabezón to Cabanilles there is a preponderance of liturgical *versos* (short contrapuntal or ornamented pieces, often based on plainchant). These *versos* were for use in music of the Mass – which involves settings of Kyrie, Gloria, Gradual, Credo, Offertory, Sanctus, Agnus Dei and Deo Gratias – and in the offices of Vespers, Compline, Matins and Lauds – including antiphons, psalms, hymns, Magnificat, Te Deum and Benedictus. The details of each ceremonial took account of particular seasons and church festivals, and in some places there were official financial penalties should the organist fail to appear.

The most comprehensive demonstration of the techniques required of a sixteenth-century Spanish organist can be seen in *Obras de música para tecla, arpa y vihuela* (compositions for keyboard and plucked string instruments) by Antonio de Cabezón (1510–66), published by his son in 1578.[1] Printed in *cifra* (figure) notation (see prefatory staves to Nos. 6, 7, 12, 13 and 14 in this volume), it includes nine settings of *Ave Maris stella*, five of *Pange lingua*, other hymns, sets of *versos*, *fabordones* and Magnificats on each of the eight tones,[2] eight sets each of four Kyries, 12 *tientos*, nine sets of *diferencias* (variations), 20 *tientos* based on liturgical works by Josquin, Clemens non Papa, Verdelot and others, and 20 *glosas* based on chansons by composers such as Willaert, Gombert and Lassus.

The term *tiento* (Spanish) or *tento* (Portuguese) normally means a contrapuntal piece for keyboard. It is the equivalent of *ricercare* or *fantasia*, and is often interchangeable with the term *obra*. The reference to *tecla, arpa y vihuela* in the title of Cabezón's collection of 1578 can be taken to mean that organ is required for the sacred works, while the variations and chanson arrangements are probably for harp, *vihuela* (a plucked string instrument similar to the guitar) or other keyboard instruments such as harpsichord and clavichord.[3] The *tientos* can be claimed, although not exclusively, for any appropriate instrument.

The layout of *versos* for the *Magnificat 8° tono* (whose plainchant appears in the Critical Commentary) enables the work to be performed in a variety of arrangements. The Magnificat consists of 12 verses, and from the score it is impossible to say whether the odd-numbered verses are to be played on the organ, with the even-numbered ones chanted, or vice versa. There are examples of vocal Magnificats by Morales and Victoria using each of these systems of alternation, and one by Robledo where even-numbered verses are set polyphonically with odd-numbered ones chanted, until the Gloria, where the reciprocal system is employed. In any case, six organ versets are sufficient for the canticle, and one may therefore be omitted from the Cabezón work, which has seven. (There is a parallel for this treatment in Titelouze's Magnificats, where alternative versets are provided for the *Deposuit* section: otherwise, the inclusion of seven *versos* by Cabezón could possibly be seen as furnishing music for the Benedictus, which requires this number). If no *verso* is omitted, the odd-numbered *versos* could be played on the organ, with the final one providing a conclusion after the *Amen*.

As most of the other composers represented in this volume can hardly be said to be well-known, some basic information about each follows here. António Carreira (c1525–c1589) was trained as a singer in the royal chapel of John III at Lisbon, later becoming chapel organist and eventually *mestre de capela*.[4] Heliadorus de Paiva (1502–52) was born in Lisbon, but spent most of his life at the Santa Cruz monastery in Coimbra.[5] Juan Bermudo (c1510–c1565) and Tomás de Santa María (d1570) are known chiefly as theorists through their published treatises. Bermudo's *Declaración de instrumentos musicales* of 1555 includes nine organ pieces 'to be played and not sung' (although published in parts) in the section dealing with performance on keyboard and plucked strings. These pieces use mainly the lower regions of the keyboard, and clearly assume the short octave arrangement in the bass. Santa María, in his *Arte de tañer fantasía* (1565), is particularly concerned with composition, and the examples here are taken from the sections on compositional technique. Again, they are not assembled in score, this being left to the player. Santa María also gives instruction on fingering, ornamentation and unequal notes when playing passages in quavers, a very early mention of the interpretation of *notes inégales*.

Luis Venegas de Henestrosa (c1510–after 1557, perhaps in Toledo) may have been the originator of the notational system employed in Cabezón's *Obras de música*. His *Libro de cifra nueva* of 1557 is the first printed book using this notation, which is explained in the introduction. It is a reasonably effective system, cheaper to print than conventional notation, and the type could be set by a printer without any musical knowledge. Venegas' *Libro* consists of well over 100 pieces, about 40 of which are by Cabezón, and includes arrangements of works by composers already mentioned in connection with Cabezón's *Obras*.[6]

Manuel Rodrigues Coelho (c1555–c1635) was organist first at Elvas cathedral, and then, from 1602 to 1633, to the Lisbon court. His *Flores de musica* (1620) is the earliest known printed keyboard music in Portugal. It contains 24 *tentos* on a larger scale than almost any works by sixteenth-century composers (the present example is by no means the longest!), sets of *versos* for hymns or canticles in the various tones, with the plainchant systematically assigned to a different voice in each *verso*, and some Magnificat and Nunc dimittis *versos* set for voice and organ.[7]

James Dalton
Oxford, 1986

1 For modern editions, see *Hispaniae schola musica sacra*, iii–iv and vii–viii and *Monumentos de la música española*, xxvii–xxix.
2 See below for a brief discussion of the church mode system.
3 Secular melodies were not unknown in church, however; organists were sometimes censured for introducing them in *tientos* and *diferencias*.
4 His compositions, all for keyboard, appear in *PC* MS 242; one is included in *Portugaliae musica*, series A, xix.
5 Three *tentos* by him are in *PC* 242; one is included in *Portugaliae musica*, xix (not one of the two printed in this anthology).
6 A modern edition is published in *Monumentos de la música española*, ii.
7 The complete work is published in *Portugaliae musica*, i and iii.

The Church Modes

The music in Vols. 4–6 of this anthology has its tonal basis in the church modes (or tones), which were evolved to classify the vast repertory of Gregorian chant. In medieval music there were eight modes, two on each pitch from d to g, the first 'authentic' and the second 'plagal'. The names, finals (that is, cadence tones) and approximate ranges of the modes are as follows:

1st mode (Dorian):
2nd mode (Hypodorian):
3rd mode (Phrygian):
4th mode (Hypophrygian):
5th mode (Lydian):
6th mode (Hypolydian):
7th mode (Mixolydian):
8th mode (Hypomixolydian):
9th mode (Aeolian):
10th mode (Hypoaeolian):
11th mode (Ionian):
12th mode (Hypoionian):

Modes 9–12 represent a Renaissance addition to the medieval classification, and are the result of an attempt to resolve the problem raised by using a system originally designed for monophonic music to accommodate polyphonic composition.

The modes, in their application to polyphonic music, clearly have much in common with modern major and minor keys, and it is not unusual for originally characteristic modal intervals to be altered chromatically. Nonetheless, some positive features are retained, as can be seen in Vol. 4 No. 1, which appears to begin in C but finishes in G. There are, too, refreshing differences of detail between mode and key: the 1st mode, for example, is very close to D minor but retains a major 6th (b♮), while the 4th mode – otherwise equivalent to the scale of E minor – has the powerful effect of a semitone between its first and second notes (e, f♮).

Modulation is generally much more restricted in modal polyphony than in major/minor tonality; this is evident in a comparison of, for example, the works of Cabanilles and Corelli, two church musicians contemporary with each other.

Modes may, however, occur in transposition, as can be seen in several pieces: Vol. 4 No. 2 and Vol. 5 No. 1, where the 3rd mode is on a instead of e; Vol. 4 No. 15 and Vol. 5 No. 4, which use the 2nd mode on g instead of d; and Vol. 5 No. 3, which employs transposition to g of the 1st mode.

Ornamentation

Advice on ornaments and their treatment is given, discursively, at various points in books by Santa María,[8] Bermudo,[9] Henestrosa[10] and, in the seventeenth century, Correa de Arauxo (who also deals with registration).[11] The following is a brief résumé of the procedures they describe.

The ornaments used in sixteenth-century Spanish keyboard music are the *quiebro* and *redoble*.[12] The simpler of the two, the *quiebro*, has the following forms (original fingerings are shown, above the stave for the right hand, below for the left):

Quiebro sencillo (simple):

Quiebro reiterado (repeated):

*very light upper auxiliary anticipating the beat.

While these make use of the main note with either upper or lower auxiliary, a further *quiebro* takes the form of a turn:

The *redoble* embodies both the turn and repetition (*reiterado*) elements:

These ornaments are not explicitly indicated in the printed text of the pieces; their use is thus left to the discretion of the performer. As regards their application, Santa María writes that the *quiebro* applies to minim, crotchet and, once in a blue moon ('por maravilla'), quaver note-values; the ornamentation occupies up to half the note, the main note being sustained for the remainder. The *quiebro* in the form of a turn, however, always occupies a minim. Ornaments can be used abundantly and with considerable freedom. They are effective at the entry of a voice, during the course of a melodic line, and particularly for decoration of a cadence. For rising passages, the *quiebro* with lower auxiliary (i.e. mordent) is often most suitable, while the upper-note shake suits descending phrases.

8 *Libro llamado Arte de tañer fantasía* (Valladolid, 1565)
9 *Declaración de instrumentos musicales* (Osuna, 1555)
10 *Libro de cifra nueva para tecla, arpa y vihuela* (Alcalá de Henares, 1557)
11 *Facultad orgánica* (Alcalá de Henares, 1626)
12 See Santa María, *op. cit.*, Vol. 1, chap. 19, ff.46v–48

Registration

The choice of stops for sixteenth-century organ music is fairly straightforward. From contemporary sources – mostly contracts[13] for organs and lists of registrations provided by organ builders – it can be inferred that using one, two or three stops at a time is the norm, while the *lleno* (chorus with mixtures: 5 or 6 stops) would be a specially grand effect reserved for saints' and other feast days. It is important to remember that the instruments were blown by human power, and the more registers used, the greater the labours of the blower. Typical registrations would be: $8' + 8'$; $8' + 4'$; $8' + 2'$; $8' + 4' + 2'$; $8' + 8' + 4'$; $8' + 8' + 2'$.

The sources say very little, however, about the type of registration appropriate to a particular style of composition. While in the sixteenth century, organ design already incorporated the principle of stops divided into bass and treble halves, with the break at $c'/c'\sharp$ (see the discussion of *medio registro* in Vol. 5), there is nothing in the surviving works of the composers represented here to indicate the use of different registrations for the two halves of the keyboard. There is no part for pedal, and it is unusual to find more than a rudimentary pedalboard on a Spanish organ; right through the eighteenth century, pedal keys were seldom more than studs to push down, their use limited to sustaining long notes in the *tiento de contras* type of composition.

The following specification,[14] that of the organ at Ciudad Rodrigo (Salamanca) Cathedral, c1580, is a characteristic example of good sixteenth-century organ design.

Bass		Treble	
Flautado	13 palmos [= 8']	Flautado	13
8a		8a	
12a		12a	
15a		15a	
Lleno	III	Lleno	III
Zimbala		Zimbala	
Dulzayna		Dulzayna	13
		Corneta magna	V

Probable compass: CDEFGA―c''', with division of stops at $c'/c'\sharp$

A horizontal Clarín (now lost) was added in about 1700.

13 See, for instance, the contract for San Juan de las Abedesas in Barcelona (1613), printed in M. A. Vente: *Die brabanter Orgel* (Amsterdam: H. J. Paris, 1958, 2/1963), p.158.
14 Printed in M. A. Vente and W. Kok: 'Organs in Spain and Portugal', *The Organ*, xxxvi, No. 143 (Jan. 1957), p.158.

Anmerkung des Herausgebers

Die vorliegende Ausgabe richtet sich an praktizierende Musiker. Alle Musikstücke erscheinen in moderner Liniennotation unter Verwendung von Violin- und Baßschlüsseln. Die Partituren dieser Ausgabe enthalten so viel Information wie möglich über die Originalquellen – in einigen Fällen bedeutend mehr, als in anderen modernen Ausgaben zu finden ist. Das Resultat ist jedoch nicht eine vereinfachte Reproduktion des Originals. Eine systematische Methode der Herausgabe wurde entwickelt, die im Folgenden zusammengefaßt wird:

1. Wenn nicht anders vermerkt, sind die Notenwerte, Taktstriche, Tonart und Taktvorzeichen des Originals beibehalten worden, ebenso die Verteilung der Noten auf die einzelnen Systeme. (In Schlußakkorden sind die Notenwerte des Originals beibehalten worden, auch da, wo nicht jede Stimme die gleiche Anzahl Schläge zählt.) Wegen der neuzeitlichen Notenlinien und

-schlüssel ist die Richtung der Notenhälse manchmal geändert worden, doch hat man versucht, die idiomatische freie Notation des Originals beizubehalten. In Tabulatur aufgezeichnete Stücke, mehrstimmige Partituren oder einzeln notierte Stimmen sind auf zwei Systeme umgeschrieben worden.

2. Die Original-Notenschlüssel und/oder -Notationen sind am Anfang von jedem Stück vermerkt, und auch anderswo, wenn nötig. Wo ein Taktvorzeichen oder eine Mensuralnotation mitten im Stück abgeändert worden ist, erscheint das Originalzeichen zwischen den Systemen.

3. Wo im Original eine ungewöhnliche Notation auftritt (z.B. schwarze ganze Noten, weiße Achtelnoten) ist die entsprechende moderne Notation verwendet und im kritischen Kommentar erwähnt worden.

4. Notenwerte, die sich über Taktstriche hinaus erstrecken, sind umgeschrieben worden unter der Verwendung von Haltebögen; im übrigen sind die Notengruppierungen des Originals (einschließlich unkonventionellen Verbindens von Achtelnoten mit Balken) beibehalten worden. Trotz dieser scheinbaren Inkonsequenz ist die Originalnotation nicht unbergründet, und eine Abänderung würde in gewissen, wenn auch nicht in allen Fällen zur Verwirrung führen. Die einzigen Ausnahmen sind frühe Quellen, und Tablatur Notation, wo jede Achtelnote oder Sechzehntelnote ein separates Fähnchen aufweist. Hier ist eine klare konventionelle Notation verwendet worden (z.B. das Verbinden von Sechzehntelnoten mit Balken in Vierergruppen).

5. In den Quellen enthaltene Vorzeichen sind unverändert übernommen worden, mit der Ausnahme, daß allfällige Erhöhungs- und Erniedrigungszeichen durch moderne Notation ersetzt worden sind (z.B. f♮ erscheint im Original oft als f♭, und e♮ als e♯). Normalerweise gilt ein Vorzeichen im Original nur für eine Note und gleich darauf folgende Wiederholungen; wo es länger zu gelten scheint, gilt ohne Vermerk des Herausgebers die heutige Konvention, wonach ein Vorzeichen für den Rest des Taktes in Kraft bleibt. (Die gleiche Regel gilt für Vorzeichen, die vom Herausgeber hinzugefügt wurden.) Alle Vorzeichen des Herausgebers sind in voller Größe in eckigen Klammern gegeben, mit der Ausnahme von aufgehobenen Vorzeichen in Tabulatur Notation, die genau genommen nicht Hinzufügungen des Herausgebers sind, da jede Note ihr eigenes Symbol hat. Einige vom Herausgeber hinzugefügte Vorzeichen sind unumgänglich infolge der verschiedenen Konventionen der alten und modernen Notation, während andere als Anregungen betrachtet werden sollten. Die zwei Arten sind aus dem Zusammenhang ersichtlich.

6. Vom Herausgeber hinzugefügte Verzierungen, Noten, Pausen und andere Einzelheiten befinden sich in eckigen Klammern. Vom Herausgeber beigefügte Bindebogen erscheinen wie folgt: ⌢. Taktstriche des Herausgebers sind zwischen den Systemen unverbunden, während bei gelegentlichem neuem Einsetzen von Taktstrichen die Originaltaktstriche in Fettdruck über den Notenlinien erscheinen. Das Einsetzen eines längeren oder kürzeren Taktes hat nicht die Absicht, den zugrunde liegenden rhythmischen Ablauf zu verändern. Hinweise auf den Verlauf der Stimmen im Original sind beibehalten worden; Zusätze des Herausgebers verwenden gestrichelte Linien.

7. Für jedes Werk, das in mehr als einer Quelle erscheint, wurde eine Hauptquelle gewählt. Sie erscheint am Anfang der Liste der Quellen für das betreffende Stück im kritischen Kommentar, und diese Version wird als Grundlage betrachtet. Allfällige Abweichungen von der Hauptquelle (z.B. wo vom Herausgeber Korrekturen angebracht wurden oder wo stellenweise eine andere Quelle vorgezogen wurde) sind im Kommentar vermerkt. Wir haben keinen Versuch unternommen, eine erschöpfende Liste von Varianten in anderen Quellen zu geben.

8. Jedes Werk ist mit einer Überschrift versehen worden. Wo Überschriften und Zuschreibungen in den Quellen enthalten sind, sind sie in der Schreibweise des Originals im Kommentar erwähnt.

Vorwort

Die iberische Orgelmusik des sechzehnten und siebzehnten Jahrhunderts weist starke liturgische Einflüsse auf. Wie in vielen Gottesdienstordnungen von Kirchen und Kathedralen festgelegt, war es die Aufgabe des Organisten, *alternatim* mit dem Chor zu spielen – d.h. eine Strophe wurde als *cantus planus* gesungen, die nächste wurde auf der Orgel gespielt, und so weiter – und in den meisten Hauptquellen von Cabezón bis Cabanilles herrschen die liturgischen *versos* (kurze kontrapunktische oder verzierte Stücke, oft in Anlehnung an den *cantus planus*) vor. Diese *versos* gehörten zur Musik der Messe mit ihren Vertonungen von Kyrie, Gloria, Graduale, Credo, Offertorium, Sanctus, Agnus Dei und Deo Gratias, und zu den Gottesdiensten der Vesper, Komplet, Mette und Laudes mit ihren Antiphonen, Psalmen, Hymnen, Magnificat, Te Deum und Benedictus. Die Einzelheiten jedes Gottesdienstes richteten sich nach den Jahreszeiten und Kirchenfesten, und an gewissen Orten gab es offizielle Geldstrafen, falls der Organist nicht erschien.

Am deutlichsten erkennt man das vom spanischen Organist des sechzehnten Jahrhunderts geforderte technische Können in *Obras de música para tecla, arpa y vihuela* (Kompositionen für Tasten- und Zupfinstrumente) von Antonio de Cabezón (1510–1566), von seinem Sohn 1578 veröffentlicht.[1] In *cifra* Notation gedruckt (siehe Einleitung zu Nr. 6, 7, 12, 13 und 14 in diesem Band) enthält dieses Werk neun Vertonungen von *Ave maris stella*, fünf von *Pange lingua*, andere Hymnen, Serien von *versos*, *fabordones* und Magnificats auf jedem der acht Töne basierend,[2] je acht Serien bestehend aus vier Kyrie, 12 *tientos*, neun Serien von *diferencias* (Variationen), 20 *tientos*, die sich auf die liturgischen Werke von Josquin, Clemens non Papa, Verdelot und anderen stützen, und 20 *glosas*, die auf Liedern von Komponisten wie Willaert, Gombert und Lassus beruhen.

Der Begriff *tiento* (spanisch) oder *tento* (portugiesisch) bezieht sich normalerweise auf ein kontrapunktisches Werk für Tasteninstrumente. Er entspricht dem *ricercare* oder der *fantasia* und ist oft dem Begriff *obra* gleichgesetzt. Die Bezeichnung *tecla, arpa y vihuela* im Titel von Cabezóns Sammlung von 1578 deutet darauf hin, daß die Orgel für geistliche Werke erforderlich ist, während die Variationen und Chansonbearbeitungen wahrscheinlich für die Harfe, *vihuela* (ein Zupfinstrument ähnlich der Gitarre) oder andere Tasteninstrumente wie z.B. Cembalo und Clavichord bestimmt sind.[3] Die *tientos* können, wenn auch nicht ausschließlich, jedem passenden Instrument zugeeignet sein.

Die Gestaltung von *versos* für das *Magnificat 8° tono* (dessen *cantus planus* im kritischen Kommentar erscheint) ist so angelegt, daß das Werk in verschiedenen Versionen gespielt werden kann. Das Magnificat besteht aus 12 Strophen, und es ist nicht ersichtlich, ob die Strophen mit ungeraden Zahlen auf der Orgel zu spielen und die mit geraden Zahlen zu singen sind, oder umgekehrt. Es gibt Beispiele von Magnificats für Singstimme von Morales und Victoria, wo jede dieser beiden Wechselmethoden verwendet wird, und eines von Robledo, wo Strophen mit geraden Zahlen mehrstimmig vertont und solche mit ungeraden Zahlen zu singen sind, bis zum Gloria, wo umgekehrt verfahren wird. Jedenfalls genügen sechs Orgelstrophen für den Lobgesang, und man kann darum von Cabezóns Werk, das sieben Strophen hat, eine auslassen. (Eine Parallele dazu findet sich in den Magnificats von Titelouze, wo der *Deposuit* Teil mit alternativen Strophen versehen ist; andernfalls könnte man die sieben *versos* von Cabezón möglicherweise so erklären, daß sie die Musik zum Benedictus liefern, welches diese Anzahl benötigt.) Wenn kein *verso* ausgelassen wird, können die mit ungeraden Zahlen auf der Orgel gespielt werden, wobei der letzte nach dem *Amen* einen Abschluß bildet.

Da die meisten anderen in diesem Band vertretenen Komponisten kaum als bekannt bezeichnet werden können, folgen hier einige wenige Angaben über jeden. António Carreira (ca. 1525–ca. 1589) wurde in der königlichen Kapelle von Johann III. in Lissabon zum Sänger ausgebildet und wurde dort später Organist und schließlich *mestre de capela*.[4] Heliadorus de Paiva (1502–1552) wurde in Lissabon geboren, verbrachte aber den größten Teil seines Lebens im Kloster Santa Cruz in Coimbra.[5] Juan Bermudo (ca. 1510–ca. 1565) und Tomás de Santa María (gest. 1570) sind hauptsächlich durch ihre veröffentlichten Abhandlungen als Theoretiker bekannt. Bermudos *Declaración de instrumentos musicales* von 1555 enthält neun Orgelstücke 'zum Spielen, nicht Singen' (obwohl in einzelnen Stimmen veröffentlicht) in dem Teil des Werkes, der sich mit der Aufführung von Werken für Tasten- und Zupfinstrumente befaßt. Diese Stücke verwenden vor allem den unteren Teil der Tastatur, und sie stützen sich auf die kleine Oktave im Baß. Santa María beschäftigt sich in *Arte de tañer fantasía* (1565) vor allem mit der Komposition, und die hier vorliegenden Beispiele sind den Teilen des Werkes entnommen, die sich mit Kompositionstechnik befassen. Auch hier sind die verschiedenen Stimmen nicht in einer Partitur vereint; dies bleibt dem Spieler überlassen. Santa María gibt auch Hinweise zum Fingersatz, zur Verzierung und bezüglich ungleicher Noten beim Spielen von Passagen mit Achtelnoten – eine sehr frühe Interpretation der *notes inégales*.

Luis Venegas de Henestrosa (ca. 1510–nach 1557, ev. in Toledo) dürfte der Erfinder des in Cabezóns *Obras de música* angewandten Notationssystems sein. Sein *Libro de cifra nueva* von 1557 ist das erste gedruckte Buch mit dieser Notation, welche im Vorwort erklärt wird. Es ist ein recht praktisches System, billiger zu drucken als die konventionelle Notation, und der Setzer braucht keinerlei musikalische Kenntnisse. Venegas' *Libro* besteht aus über 100 Stücken, etwa 40 davon sind von Cabezón, und enthält auch Bearbeitungen von Werken von Komponisten, die im Zusammenhang mit Cabezóns *Obras* bereits erwähnt worden sind.[6]

Manuel Rodrigues Coelho (ca. 1555–ca. 1635) war zuerst Organist der Kathedrale von Elvas und dann, von 1602–33, am Hofe in Lissabon. Sein *Flores de musica* (1620) ist, soviel man weiß, die erste gedruckte Musik für Tasteninstrumente aus Portugal. Das Werk enthält 24 *tentos* von größerem Umfang als fast alle Werke anderer Komponisten des 16. Jahrhunderts (das vorliegende Beispiel ist bei weitem nicht das längste Stück!), Serien von *versos* für Hymnen oder Lobgesänge in verschiedenen Tonarten, mit dem *cantus planus* in jeder *verso* systematisch einer anderen Stimme zugewiesen, und einige Magnificat- und Nunc dimittis *versos* für Gesang und Orgel.[7]

James Dalton
Oxford, 1986

1 Für moderne Ausgaben siehe *Hispaniae schola musica sacra*, iii–iv und vii–viii und *Monumentos de la música española*, xxvii–xxix.
2 Siehe unten für eine kurze Einführung in das System des kirchlichen Modus.
3 Profane Melodien waren jedoch in der Kirche nicht unbekannt; Organisten wurden manchmal kritisiert, wenn sie solche in *tientos* und *diferencias* aufnahmen.
4 Seine Werke, alle für Tasteninstrumente, erscheinen in *PC* 242; eines ist in *Portugaliae musica*, Serie A, xix, enthalten.
5 Drei seiner *tentos* sind in *PC* 242; eines befindet sich in *Portugaliae musica*, xix (in der vorliegenden Ausgabe nicht enthalten).
6 Eine moderne Ausgabe ist in *Monumentos de la música española*, ii, veröffentlicht.
7 Das ganze Werk erscheint in *Portugaliae musica*, i und iii.

Die kirchlichen Modi

Die Musik in den Bänden 4–6 dieser Anthologie beruht klanglich auf den kirchlichen Modi (oder Tonarten), welche entwickelt wurden, um das große Repertoire des gregorianischen Gesanges zu kennzeichnen. Die mittelalterliche Musik kannte acht Modi, zwei für jede Tonhöhe von d bis g, der erste 'authentisch' und der zweite 'plagal'. Die Namen, Finales (d.h. die Kadenztöne) und die ungefähren Tonumfänge der Modi sind die folgenden:

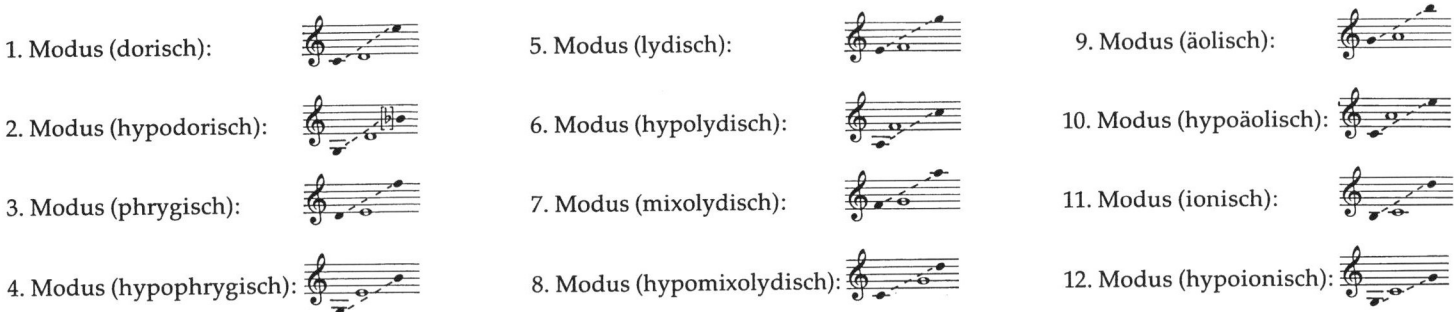

Die Modi 9–12 sind ein Beitrag der Renaissance zur mittelalterlichen Klassifizierung. Sie entstanden aus dem Versuch, das Problem zu lösen, das sich daraus ergab, daß man ein ursprünglich für homophone Musik entworfenes System für polyphone Kompositionen verwendete.

Zweifellos entsprechen die Modi in ihrer Anwendung auf die polyphone Musik in mancher Hinsicht den modernen Dur- und Molltonarten, und es ist nicht ungewöhnlich, daß die ursprünglich charakteristischen modalen Tonabstände verändert wurden. Trotzdem verbleiben aber einige typische Merkmale, wie aus Nr. 1 im Band 4 ersichtlich ist, welche in C-Dur anzufangen scheint, aber in G-Dur endet. Es gibt auch erfrischende kleine Unterschiede zwischen der Kirchentonart und moderner Tonart: Der erste Modus ist z.B. sehr ähnlich wie d-moll, behält aber eine 6. Note in Dur (h), während der 4. Modus einen wirkungsvollen Halbton zwischen seiner ersten und zweiten Note aufweist (e, f♮), obwohl er sonst mit e-moll identisch ist.

Die Modulation ist allgemein in der modalen Polyphonie beschränkter als in den Dur und Molltonarten. Das ist z.B. aus einem Vergleich der Werke von Cabanilles und Corelli ersichtlich, zwei kirchlichen Musikern die Zeitgenossen waren.

Die Modi können jedoch auch in Transpositionen erscheinen, wie aus verschiedenen Stücken hervorgeht: Band 4, Nr. 2 und Band 5, Nr. 1, wo der 3. Modus auf a basiert statt auf e; Band 4, Nr. 15 und Band 5, Nr. 4, welche den 2. Modus auf g statt auf d gestützt verwenden; und Band 5, Nr. 3, mit einer Transposition des 1. Modus auf g.

Ornamentierung

Ausgiebige Ratschläge in Bezug auf die Ornamentierung und ihre Interpretation finden sich an verschiedenen Stellen in den Büchern von Santa María,[8] Bermudo,[9] Henestrosa[10] und – im 17. Jahrhundert – Correa de Arauxo (der sich auch mit der Registrierung befaßt).[11] Hier folgt eine kurze Zusammenfassung der beschriebenen Anleitungen.

Die in der spanischen Tastenmusik des 16. Jahrhunderts verwendeten Verzierungen sind *quiebro* und *redoble*.[12] Die einfachere der beiden, der *quiebro*, weist die folgenden Varianten auf. (Der OriginalFingersatz für die rechte Hand befindet sich über den Notenlinien, für die linke Hand unter den Notenlinien.)

Quiebro sencillo (einfach):

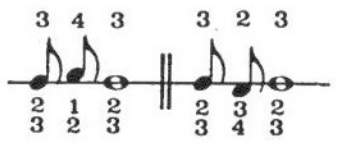

Quiebro reiterado (wiederholt):

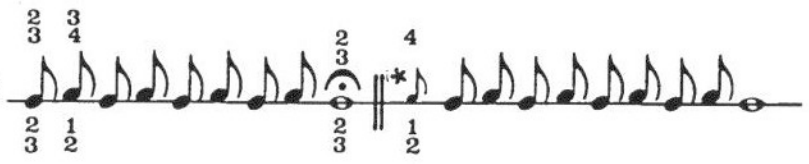

*Sehr kurzer Vorschlag von oben, den Takt einleitend.

Während sich die obigen Verzierungen auf die Hauptnote stützen mit einer oberen oder unteren Nebennote weist ein weiterer *quiebro* einen Nachschlag auf:

Der *redoble* vereint den Nachschlag und die Wiederholung (*reiterado*):

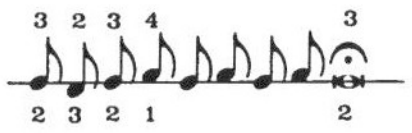

Diese Verzierungen sind im gedruckten Text zu den Stücken nicht ausdrücklich erwähnt. Ihre Verwendung bleibt also dem Vortragenden überlassen. Bezüglich ihrer Anwendung schreibt Santa María, daß der *quiebro* sich auf die halbe und die Viertelnote bezieht, und in seltenen Fällen ('*por maravilla*') auch auf Achtelnoten. Die Verzierung nimmt höchstens die Hälfte der Note in Anspruch und wird durch die Hauptnote fortgesetzt. Der *quiebro* mit Nachschlag wird aber immer auf halbe Noten angewandt. Verzierungen können reichlich und mit beträchtlicher Freiheit verwendet werden. Sie sind wirkungsvoll vor dem Eintritt einer Stimme, im Verlaufe einer melodischen Sequenz und besonders zur Verzierung einer Kadenz. Für aufsteigende Passagen ist oft der *quiebro* mit einer unteren Nebennote (d.h. Mordent) am besten geeignet, während sich der Triller mit der oberen Nebennote für absteigende Passagen eignet.

---

8 *Libro llamado Arte de tañer fantasía* (Valladolid, 1565).
9 *Declaración de instrumentos musicales* (Osuna, 1555).
10 *Libro de cifra nueva para tecla, arpa y vihuela* (Alcalá de Henares, 1557).
11 *Facultad orgánica* (Alcalá de Henares, 1626).
12 Siehe Santa María, *op. cit.*, Band 1, Kapitel 19, ff.46v–48.

Registrierung

Die Wahl der Register für Orgelmusik des 16. Jahrhunderts ist recht unkompliziert. Aus zeitgenössischen Quellen – vorwiegend Aufträge[13] zum Orgelbau und vom Orgelbauer aufgestellte Registrierungslisten – ist ersichtlich, daß in der Regel ein, zwei oder drei Register auf einmal verwendet worden sind, während der *lleno* (Chor mit Mixturen: 5 oder 6 Register), für die Tage der Heiligen und andere Festtage reserviert, eine besonders großartige Wirkung erzielte. Man darf aber nicht vergessen, daß Instrumente damals mit menschlicher Kraft geblasen wurden, und je mehr Register gebraucht werden, desto größer ist der Kraftaufwand des Bläsers. Typische Registrierungen wären: 8′ + 8′; 8′ + 4′; 8′ + 2′; 8′ + 4′ + 2′; 8′ + 8′ + 4′; 8′ + 8′ + 2′.

In den Quellen steht aber sehr wenig über die einem bestimmten Kompositionsstil angemessene Registrierung. Während im 16. Jahrhundert der Orgelbau bereits das Prinzip der Zweiteilung in Baß und Diskantregister kannte, mit einer Teilung bei c'/c'♯ (siehe Beschreibung von *medio registro* im Band 5), weist in den noch existierenden Werken der hier vertretenen Komponisten nichts darauf hin, daß für die zwei Hälften der Tastatur verschiedene Registrierungen eingesetzt wurden. Es gibt keine Stimme für das Pedal, und meistens findet man an einer spanischen Orgel nur ein rudimentäres Pedalwerk. Während des ganzen 18. Jahrhunderts waren Pedaltasten kaum mehr als Knöpfe zum Hinunterdrücken; ihr Zweck beschränkte sich auf das Aushalten langer Noten in Kompositionen von der Art des *tiento de contras*.

Die folgenden technischen Angaben zur Orgel der Kathedrale von Ciudad Rodrigo (Salamanca), ca. 1580,[14] sind ein typisches Beispiel guten Orgelbaus im 16. Jahrhundert.

Baß		*Diskant*	
Flautado	13 palmos [= 8′]	Flautado	13
8a		8a	
12a		12a	
15a		15a	
Lleno	III	Lleno	III
Zimbala		Zimbala	
Dulzayna		Dulzayna	13
		Corneta magna	V

Wahrscheinlicher Tonumfang: CDEFGA_____c''', mit Teilung der Register bei c'/c'♯

Ein horizontaler Clarín (heute nicht mehr vorhanden) wurde ca. 1700 hinzugefügt.

---

13 Siehe z.B. den Auftrag für San Juan de las Abedesas in Barcelona (1613), wiedergegeben in M. A. Vente: *Die brabanter Orgel* (Amsterdam: J. A. Paris, 1958, 2/1963), S.158.
14 Abgedruckt in M. A. Vente und W. Kok: 'Organs in Spain and Portugal', *The Organ*, xxxvi, No. 143 (Jan. 1957), S.158.

1. Tento do 8° tom

ANTÓNIO CARREIRA (c1525 - c1589)

© 1987 by Faber Music Ltd

This music is copyright. Photocopying is illegal.

2. Tento do 3º tom

HELIADORUS DE PAIVA (c1500 - 1552)

3. Tento do 4º tom

HELIADORUS DE PAIVA (c1500 - 1552)

4. *Veni creator spiritus*

JUAN BERMUDO *(c1510 - ?1565)*

5. Pange lingua

JUAN BERMUDO *(c1510 - ?1565)*

6. *Tiento de 5° tono*

ANONYMOUS *(1557)*

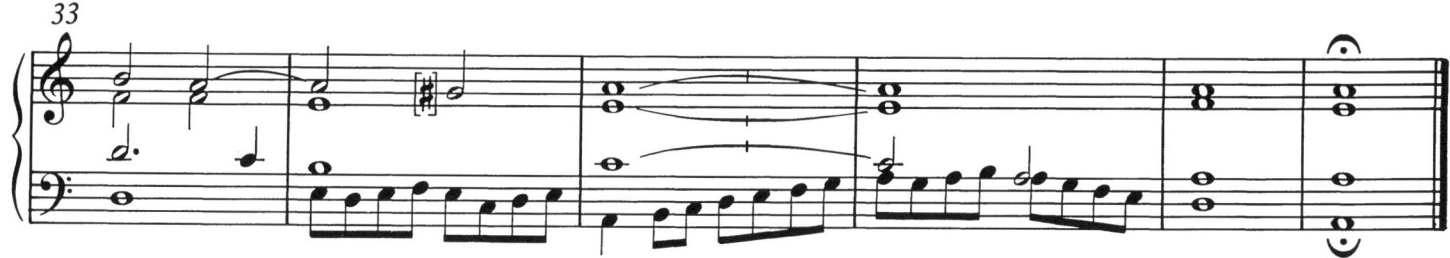

7. Tiento de 7° tono super Philomena

FRANCISCO FERNÁNDEZ PALERO *(d1597)*

8. *Del modo de tañer a corcheas*

TOMÁS DE SANTA MARÍA (d?1570)

9. *Fuga a dos voces*

TOMÁS DE SANTA MARÍA *(d?1570)*

10. *Fuga a tres voces*

TOMÁS DE SANTA MARÍA *(d?1570)*

11. *Fuga a cuatro voces*

TOMÁS DE SANTA MARÍA *(d?1570)*

12. *Beata viscera Mariae virginis*

ANTONIO DE CABEZÓN *(1510 - 1566)*

13. *Versos del 8° tono de Magnificat*

ANTONIO DE CABEZÓN *(1510 - 1566)*

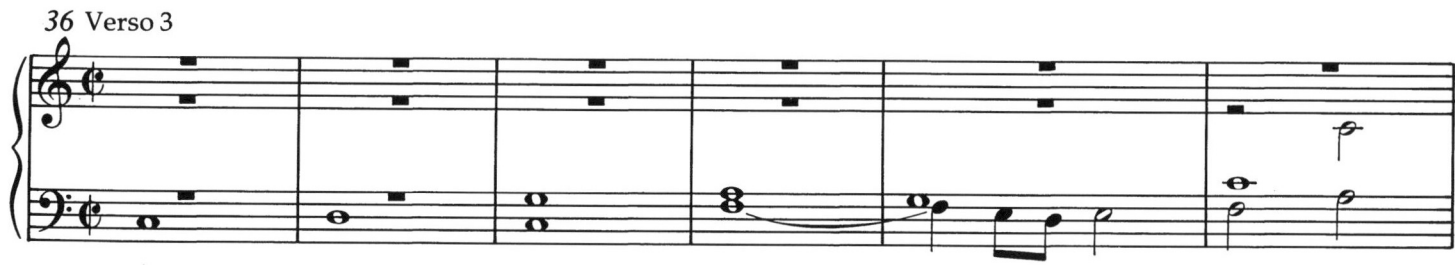

14. *Tiento sobre Cum sancto spiritu*

ANTONIO DE CABEZÓN *(1510-1566)*

15. *Versos do 3° tom*

MANUEL RODRIGUES COELHO *(c1555 - 1635)*

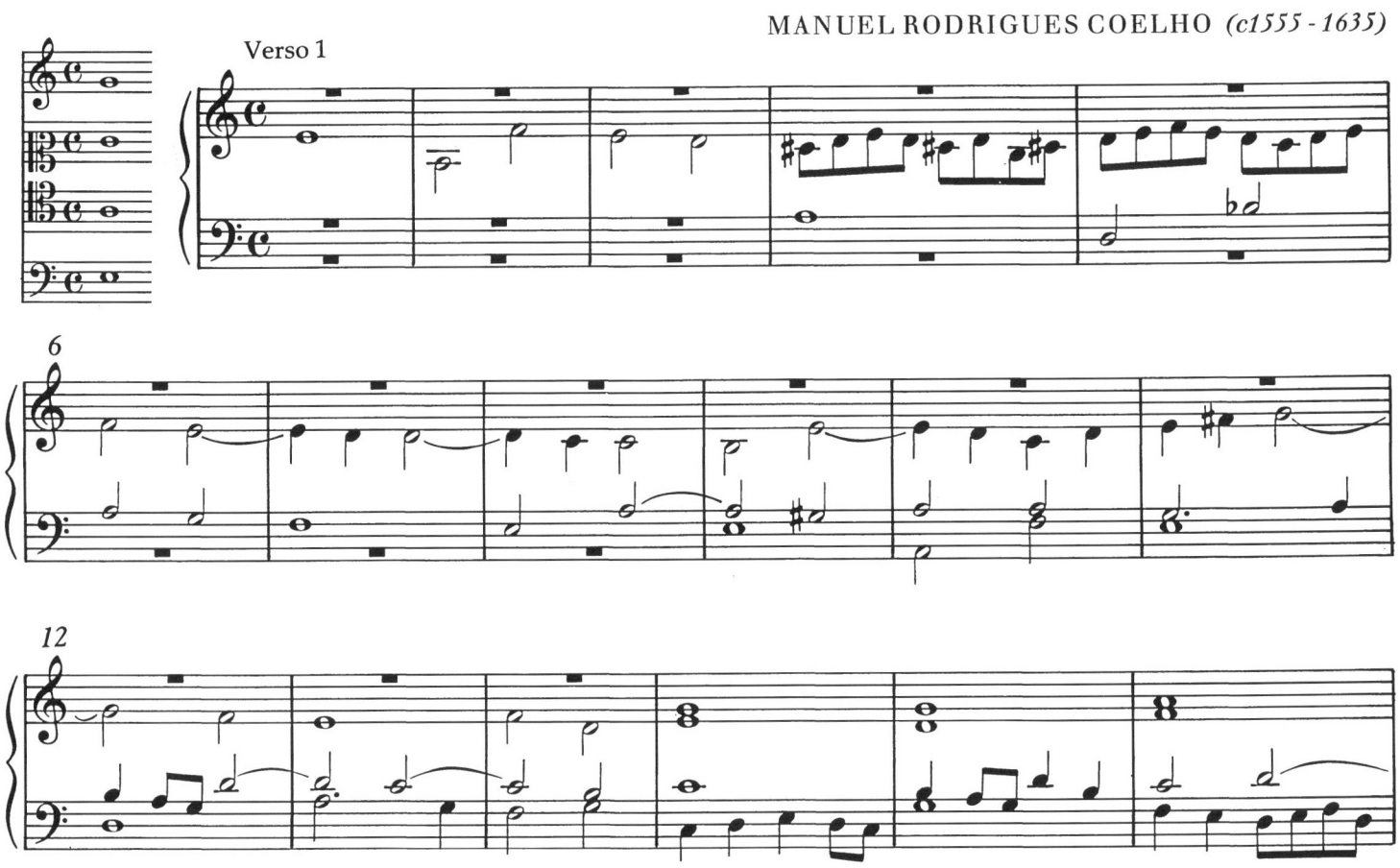

16. *Tento do 2° tom*

MANUEL RODRIGUES COELHO *(c1555 - 1635)*

Critical Commentary

Sources are listed for each piece, together with original titles and/or ascriptions where present. Where there is more than one source, the first listed represents the main source for the edition (see Editorial Procedure, §7); any deviations from the main source are detailed in the Commentary below.

The following RISM sigla are used to indicate the libraries in which sources are located:
- EMn – Madrid: Biblioteca nacional
- PBRp – Braga: Biblioteca pública e arquivo distrital
- PC – Biblioteca geral, Universidade de Coimbra

The following abbreviations are used:
- S – soprano
- A – alto
- T – tenor
- B – bass
- lh – left hand
- rh – right hand

Pitches are notated as follows:

C′-B′ C-B c-b c′-b′ c″-b″ c‴-b‴

32 T 7-9 ♩♫ means that in bar 32 the seventh, eighth and ninth notes of the tenor part are a crotchet and two quavers in the source; 4 rh middle voice 2, 3 f′♯ g′♯ means that in bar 4, right hand, middle voice, the second and third notes are middle octave F♯ and G♯ in the source.

1. **Tento do 8° tom**
   PC M.242, f.39v. [untitled] *Ca*
   30–46 S written one bar too early (29–45)

2. **Tento do 3° tom**
   PC M.242, f.97. [untitled] *Heliadorus*

3. **Tento do 4° tom**
   PC M.242, f.87v. [untitled] *Heliadorus*
   65 T c / 79 B 2 c ♩ in addition to A

4. **Veni creator spiritus**
   Juan Bermudo: *Declaración de instrumentos musicales* (1555), f.CXIXv. *Veni creator spiritus*

5. **Pange lingua**
   Declaración de instrumentos musicales (1555), f.CXX. *Pange lingua*

6. **Tiento de 5° tono**
   Luis Venegas de Henestrosa: *Libro de Cifra nueva / para tecla, harpa, y vihuela . . .* (1557), f.30v. *Otro quinto tono* [pencilled on copy (EMn, R.598):] *Verso de Morales glosado de Palero*
   12 S 1 g′ / 15 A 1 a / 20 S g′ / 22 T a o

7. **Tiento de 7° tono super Philomena**
   Libro de Cifra nueva . . . (1557), f.32. *Super Philomena, Septimo tono;* [in contents list:] *Septimo tono Francisco fernandez Palero*
   7 S 1 e″ / 11 B 1 g / 14 S 1 f′ / 29 B F / 43 S 3 c″ / 46 S 2 f′ / 47 B 1 g / 50 S d″♯ / 63 T 1 g / 68 A 4 a

8. **Del modo de tañer a corcheas**
   Tomás de Santa María: *Libro llamado / Arte de tañer Fantasia, asi para Tecla / como para Vihuela, y todo instrumēto . . .* (1565), Vol.II, f.63. [Title is original, but applies to the chapter dealing with rhythmic interpretation]
   All quavers have separate stems in the original.

9. **Fuga a dos voces**
   . . . Arte de tañer Fantasia . . ., Vol.II, f.67v. *A duo;* [chapter heading:] *Del modo de hazer fugas*

10. **Fuga a tres voces**
    . . . Arte de tañer Fantasia . . ., Vol.II, f.68. *Fuga a tres vozes* [chapter heading as for No.9]

11. **Fuga a cuatro voces**
    . . . Arte de tañer Fantasia . . ., Vol.II, f.81. [untitled; chapter heading:] *Del modo de taner los passos a concierto a quatro voces;* [heading on f.81:] *Del modo de tañer los passos sueltos*

12. **Beata viscera Mariae virginis**
    Antonio de Cabezón: *Obras de musica para tecla arpa y vihuela* (1578), f.4. *Beata viscera mariae. Canto llano;* [in contents list:] *Beata viscera Mariae canto llano con el / baxo a tres*
    8 rh 1 f

13. **Versos del 8° tono de Magnificat**
    Obras de musica . . ., f.39. *Versos del octavo tono;* [in contents list: section heading] *Comiençan los versos de Magnificat / sobre todos los ocho tonos;* [title] *Siete versos del octavo tono*

    Magnificat chant (see Introduction):

    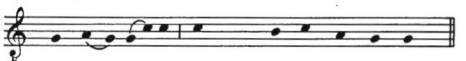

    1. Ma-gni-fi-cat   anima me-a Do-mi-num.

    2. Et   ex - sultavit spiritus   me -   us
    3. Qui - a   respexit humilitatem ancillae su -   ae:
    4. Qui - a   fecit mihi magna qui   potens   est:
    5. Et   mi - sericordia ejus a progenie in pro- ge-ni- es
    6. Fe -   cit   potentiam in bracchio   su -   o:
    7. De -   po - suit potentes de   se -   de:
    8. E -   su - rientes implevit   bo -   nis;
    9. Su -   sce -pit Israel puerum   su -   um,
    10. Si -   cut locutus est ad patres   no -   stros,
    11. Glo - ria Patri et   Fi -li-   o,
    12. Si -   cut erat in principio et nunc, et   sem -   per,

    in Deo salu -   -ta - ri me - o.
    ecce enim ex hoc beatam
       me dicent omnes gene -   - ra - ti - o - nes.
    et sanctum   no- men e - jus.
    timen -   - ti - bus e - um.
    dispersit superbos mente   cor - dis su - i.
    et exal -   - ta - vit hu miles.
    et divites dimi -   - sit i - na - nes.
    recordatus misericor -   - di - ae su - ae.
    Abraham et semini e -   - jus in sae - cula.
    et Spiri -   - tu - i san - cto.
    et in saecula saecu   - lo - rum. A - men.

14. **Tiento sobre Cum sancto spiritu**
    Obras de musica . . ., f.68. [in contents list:] *Tiento sobre el cum sancto spiritu, de / beata virgine de Iusquin*

15. **Versos do 3° tom**
    Manuel Rodrigues Coelho: *Flores / de Musica / pera o instrumento de / Tecla, & Harpa* (1620), f.201v. [v.1] *Versos do terceiro tom sobre o canto chão de tiple;* [v.2] *Segundo verso do terceiro tom sobre o canto chão de contralto;* [v.3] *Terceiro Verso do terceiro tom sobre o canto chão do tenor;* [v.4] *Quarto Verso do terceiro tom sobre o canto chão do contrabaixo*
    Also occurs in PBRp Ms.964, f.199
    All quavers and semiquavers have separate stems in the original.
    20 B 2 b / 59 S 1–4 originally notated ♩.³ ♪ ♩.³ ♪

16. **Tento do 2° tom**
    Flores / de Musica . . ., f.15. [contents list:] *Tento de segundo tom porb. mol*
    Also occurs in PBRp Ms.964, f.163v
    All quavers and semiquavers have separate stems in the original.
    204 B 1 redundant ♭ / 231 A 1 redundant ♭